First edition for the United States and Canada published
in 2012 by Barron's Educational Series, Inc.

First published in 2012 by Wayland, Hachette Children's Books,
338, Euston Rd., London NW1 3BH

Concept design: Kate Buxton
Series design: Paul Cherrill

All inquiries should be addressed to:
Barron's Educational Series, Inc.
250 Wireless Boulevard, Hauppauge, New York 11788
www.barronseduc.com

ISBN: 978-1-4380-0188-3

Library of Congress Control No.: 2012937495

Printed in China

Manufactured by: Shenzhen Wing King Tong Paper Products Co. Ltd., Guangdong, China
Date of Manufacture: August 2012

9 8 7 6 5 4 3 2 1

I Miss My Pet

A FIRST LOOK AT WHEN A PET DIES

PAT THOMAS
ILLUSTRATED BY LESLEY HARKER

BARRON'S

Pets come in all shapes and sizes.
There are big ones...

...and small ones.

Some have fur, some have feathers
and some have scales.

Whether your pet
walks or flies or swims
doesn't matter.

Each pet is a special friend that brings
us happiness every day.

Some people's pets have lived with them for so long it can be hard to remember a time when they weren't there.

We all want out pets to be with us forever.

But just like all living things, pets sometimes die.

Death is a natural part of life. We all grow
and change, and one day we all die.

Even though it is natural when someone,
or something, you love dies, it is always very
sad—and it always seems very unfair.

What about you?

Did you have a special pet? What was its name?

What has happened to it?

Pets die for the same
reasons that people do.

?

They can get sick,
or have an accident,
or just be very old.

If your pet is sick, sometimes
special doctors called
veterinarians can help
it get better.

16

But even when a veterinarian tries very hard, there are times when nothing anyone can do can help your pet to get better.

17

Sometimes we can be with
our pets before they die
and comfort them
and say goodbye.

But other times death
is a sad surprise.

Whatever happens, remember that once your pet dies, it is at peace and no longer in pain or distress.

Most people think of their
pets as members of
their family.

They can be the first thing we see in the
morning and the last thing we see at night.

We talk to them, and play with them, and take care of them just like we do other family members.

What about you?

How did you take care of your pet?
What sort of things did your pet enjoy doing?

When your pet dies, it is normal to feel sad, lonely, angry, or confused.

Whatever you feel, it can help to talk about it to your family and friends.

You may wonder why your pet
had to die and if it will come back.
But even though death is forever, your
sad feelings will not last that long.

It can help you feel better to find special ways to remember your pet. Everyone does this in a different way.

What about you?

What special ways can you think of to celebrate the life of your pet?

What would make you feel better right now?

Sometimes people have special ceremonies or write poems, sing songs or make videos or scrapbooks.

Sometimes they just talk about all the fun they had with their pet when it was alive.

Saying goodbye in a way that makes you and your family feel better can bring comfort and peace to everyone.

And it can help you to remember
how much you loved your pet—
and how much they loved you.

HOW TO USE THIS BOOK

Children learn a great deal about life and death from their pets. A child who is involved in caring for an animal, treating it with kindness and love, and commitment to its needs, is learning to treat other people that way too. Similarly the death of a pet is a lesson in letting go and saying goodbye.

This book provides opportunities to stop and talk about things. Before reading it to your child, take a moment to read through the text and be clear of your own feelings about, and reactions to, the death of your pet and those of your child.

The death of a pet can be a child's first experience of a loss of this kind. Some recover quite quickly and others take time to adjust. It's important to see grief as a process—not an event—and let your child grieve in a way that is appropriate for their age and level of understanding.

Tell the truth. However your pet dies, be honest with your child. Don't say "the dog ran away" or "the bird went on a trip." It is unlikely to make the sadness any less bearable and later on down the line can lead to a sense of betrayal and anger that they were lied to.

Talk about your own grief. If your child sees you allowing grief to be a part of your life, then they too will feel able to allow themselves to grieve.

Children have lots of questions after a pet dies. Try to answer them as honestly and simply as you can. If your child wants to know what happens to a pet after death, draw on your own philosophical understanding or religious beliefs about such things. If you don't know, just say "I don't know." Perhaps invite your child to speculate on what happens after death.

Some parents find it hard to understand why a child might grieve a pet more than the loss of, for example, a distant relative. Try to remember that, for a young child, a pet that has been in their life every day is more "real" than a relative they rarely see.

Consider a family burial ceremony. Write a poem or prayer together, or offer thoughts on what the pet meant to each of you. You can also plant a tree or other living memorial in the pet's name, keep photos around the house and share stories of your family's enjoyment of your pet. Help your child understand that the animal you loved lives on in your memories.

In some cases the death of a pet may bring up feelings of other painful losses in the child's life. Similarly, young children who lack the language to express themselves may show anger or aggression or regressive behavior such as bed-wetting or thumb sucking. Try to be sensitive to this and, where necessary, let teachers and caregivers know what is going on.

Teachers are in an excellent position to help children think about our relationship to animals—from personal pets to those in zoos and in the wild. Teachers may consider making a book or scrapbook about all the pets that the children in the class have. Many classes have pets that the children take turns caring for. This can be a springboard for discussions and projects about our personal pets and our experiences with them. If a class pet dies, encourage the children to talk about it and to take part in organizing a ceremony to say goodbye.

BOOKS TO READ

For Children

My Pet Died (Let's Make a Book About It)
Rachel Biale (Ten Speed Press, 1997)

The Forever Dog
Bill Cochran and Dan Andreasen
(Harper Collins, 2007)

For the Love of Emrys
Barbara Ann Simone (Get Published, 2011)

Saying Goodbye to Lulu
Corinne Demas and Ard Hoyt (Little Brown, 2009)

Badger's Parting Gifts
Susan Varley (Picture Lions, 1992)

For Adults

**Pet Loss: A Thoughtful Guide for Adul
and Children**
Herbert A Nieburg and Arlene Fischer
(Harper Perennial, 1996)

**The Loss of a Pet: A Guide to Coping
the Grieving Process When a Pet Dies**
Wallace Sife, PhD (Howell Book House, 2005)

RESOURCES FOR ADULTS

Society for Companion Animal Studies (UK)
Online services, leaflets and books about
pet loss and advice on pet memorials:
http://www.scas.org.uk

American Veterinary Medical Association (US)
A range of online resources for dealing with pet loss:
http://www.avma.org/care4pets/default.htm

**Consult your local veterinarian for local pet
loss helplines and burial services**